Whose Birthday Is It?

Written and Illustrated by
Linda L. Lile

A-LU Publishing, Traverse City, MI

Published by
A-LU Publishing
Traverse City, MI

Publisher's Cataloging-in-Publication Data
Lile, Linda L.

Whose birthday is it? / written and illustrated by Linda L. Lile. –
Traverse City, MI : A-LU Pub., 2018.

p. ; cm.

Summary: On an exciting December morning, Nonnie's grandchildren come over to help prepare for a special celebration.

ISBN13: 978-0-981-70923-9

1. Grandparents—Juvenile fiction. 2. Grandchildren—Juvenile fiction.
3. Christmas—Juvenile fiction. I. Title.

PZ7.1.L55 2018
[E]--dc23 2018938232

Project coordination by Jenkins Group, Inc.
www.BookPublishing.com

Design by Eric Tufford

Printed in Malaysia by Tien Wah Press (PTE) Limited,
First Printing, June 2018

22 21 20 19 18 • 5 4 3 2 1

For unto us a child is born,
unto us a son is given:
and the government shall be
upon his shoulder:
and his name shall be called
Wonderful, Counsellor,
The mighty God,
The everlasting Father,
The Prince of Peace.

Isaiah 9:6

Dedicated to God with gratitude
for His favor upon my life.

To Glen, my love always and forever.

To my children and grandchildren
for their love and inspiration.

A special heartfelt thank you to all those
who have been part of my journey.

Author's Note

Being a grandparent is a wonderful blessing, and it warms my heart when my grandchildren call me Nonnie. As the author of children's books, I enjoy sharing my experiences, and I want other grandparents to be included in the fun, too.

To help that along, the word "Nonnie" is faded throughout *Whose Birthday Is It?* to encourage readers to replace it with the name their own grandchildren have given them.

As the sun begins to rise on this crisp December morning, Nonnie is busy in the kitchen. Soon, her countertops are covered with flour and sugar and the sink piled high with mixing bowls, measuring cups, and dirty pans.

This will be an exciting day for Nonnie because her grandchildren are coming over to help prepare for a special celebration.

The grandchildren love helping their Nonnie bake, and they know she will have flour everywhere, sometimes even on the tip of her nose. It's always so much fun!

While waiting for her grandchildren to arrive, Nonnie dances around the kitchen singing Christmas carols and adding the final drops of food coloring to the frosting. Then she sets the table in the dining room with brightly colored sprinkles and small bowls of frosting.

She is just setting the last bowl down when...

Knock, knock. Nonnie stops singing and calls, "Come in!"

There is no answer, so she sets the bowl on the table, grabs a towel to wipe her hands, and walks to the door.

"Surprise, Nonnie!" Parker yells as he and his older brother Austin step inside.

"Oh, my! You boys surprised me!" Nonnie smiles as she helps the boys remove their coats, boots, and mittens.

Parker turns, wrapping his tiny arms around her, squeezing as hard as he can. He is almost four years old and very excited. Big brother Austin is five and just as eager.

As Nonnie heads toward the table, Parker stops, saying, "Wait, Nonnie, did you forget our snack?"

"That's right! Your mommy said you boys were hungry when she called to say you were on the way!" exclaims Nonnie.

Austin and Parker are lucky to live right next door to their grandparents.

After clearing a spot on the table, Nonnie brings in a warm plate of sugar cookies and two glasses of milk from the kitchen. The boys quickly climb into their chairs and dig in. They love eating cookies.

Just then, Nonnie hears another knock at the door.

Before she can check to see who it is, Abby and Piper push open the door. Abby, Nonnie's oldest grandchild at age six, is excited that her little cousin Piper's family is visiting for the holiday. Abby is especially delighted that she gets to help take care of Piper, who is just three years old.

Like the boys, the girls greet Nonnie with a big hug once they finish hanging their coats on the hook.

Austin invites the girls to the table for cookies and milk.

Piper hurries to join in, and Abby follows after her little cousin.

The older children finish eating first. They help Nonnie by carrying their glasses and plates to the already full sink in the kitchen.

Once Parker and Piper finish their snack, they wait patiently to begin decorating cookies, but they are having trouble: it is hard to decide which of the many shapes Nonnie has made to frost first!

The time to decorate cookies has come. Soon, Nonnie and her grandchildren have made red bells, yellow stars, green Christmas trees, and rainbow-colored reindeer. The sprinkles cover the table and even roll onto the floor. Nonnie is surprised to see that some of the sprinkles actually land on the cookies!

Parker dabs frosting on Piper's nose to make everyone laugh. When Austin decides to bite the hooves off his reindeer, they all laugh even more. When the cookies are all decorated, Nonnie suggests they take a break and sing Christmas songs. Of course, Austin picks "Rudolph, the No-Hooved Reindeer"!

When they finish singing, Nonnie clears the table and tells the children she needs help with another very special project. She disappears into the kitchen and returns with a large undecorated cake.

"This cake is for a birthday celebration," Nonnie says, carefully placing the cake on the table.

Parker looks puzzled. He asks, "Nonnie, whose birthday is it?"

Holding her Bible closely, Nonnie pulls a chair next to the table and sits down.

"Tomorrow is Christmas," says Austin. "Who has a birthday on Christmas?" he prompts.

"The Baby Jesus was born on Christmas," Abby says.

"You are right!" says Nonnie. "Jesus was born on Christmas, and He is the reason we celebrate!"

Abby nods at her younger cousins. "Christmas isn't just about us getting presents," she explains.

While the children frost the special cake, Nonnie reads the story of the Christ Child's birth. The children listen quietly to the beautiful words about Mary and Joseph and the angels and shepherds. They are excited to hear about the amazing star that leads the three wise men to the Baby Jesus.

They are also delighted to know that Christmas is Jesus's birthday and that, as a family, they will gather to celebrate this child who was sent to save the world.

After Nonnie closes her Bible, Piper asks, "Nonnie, can we make a special birthday cake for Jesus every Christmas?"

"Yes, of course," says Nonnie. "I am so blessed to share the true meaning of Christmas with all of you!"

For a true understanding of this special birth, I invite you to read **Luke 2:4–20**

4 And Joseph also went up from Galilee, out of the city of Nazareth, into the city Judaea, unto the city of David, which is called Bethlehem; (because he was of the house and lineage of David:)

5 To be taxed with Mary his espoused wife, being great with child.

6 And so it was, that, while they were there, the days were accomplished that she should be delivered.

7 And she brought forth her firstborn son, and wrapped him in swaddling clothes, and laid him in a manger; because there was no room for them in the inn.

8 And there were in the same country shepherds abiding in the fields, keeping watch over their flock by night.

9 And, lo, the angel of the Lord came upon them, and the glory of the Lord shone round about them: and they were sore afraid.

10 And the angel said unto them, Fear not: for, behold, I bring you good tidings of great joy, which shall be to all people.

11 For unto you is born this day in the city of David a Saviour, which is Christ the Lord.

12 And this shall be a sign unto you; Ye shall find the babe wrapped in swaddling clothes, lying in a manger.

13 And suddenly there was with the angel a multitude of the heavenly host praising God, and saying,

14 Glory to God in the highest, and on earth peace, good will toward men.

15 And it came to pass, as the angels were gone away from them into heaven, the shepherds said one to another, Let us now go even unto Bethlehem, and see this thing which is come to pass, which the Lord hath made known unto us.

16 And they came with haste, and found Mary, and Joseph, and the babe lying in a manger.

17 And when they had seen it, they made known abroad the saying which was told them concerning this child.

18 And all they that heard it wondered at those things which were told them by the shepherds.

19 But Mary kept all these things, and pondered them in her heart.

20 And the shepherds returned, glorifying and praising God for all the things that they had heard and seen, as it was told unto them.

Authorized King James Version (ZonderVan Publishing House)